THE RENEWING MIND

Devotions for the Journey to Recovery and Life Transformation
Vol. 1

RACHELE A. DIXIE, MA, MDiv

THE RENEWING MIND

Devotions for the Journey to
Recovery and Life Transformation - Vol. 1

HOV Publishing a division of HOV, LLC.
www.hovpub.com
hopeofvision@gmail.com

Cover Design: HOV Design Solutions
Editor/Proofreader: Amy Owens for Clarity Communications

Write the Author Rachele A. Dixie at:
Email: destinee.project@gmail.com

For more information about special discounts for bulk purchases, please contact destinee.project@gmail.com

ISBN: 978-1-955107-84-6 Paperback
978-1-955107-83-9 eBook

10 9 8 7 6 5 4 3 2 1

Printed in the United States of America

DEDICATION

I want to first dedicate this devotional to my mother, Cordelia E. Dixie, who has continuously prayed for me through every facet of my walk with the Lord. I thank her for always supporting me and seeing the best in me even when I did not see it in myself. I also dedicate this to my loving twin sister, Dr. Michele Renee Wells, who is my voice of reason and inspiration to press further into what I am purposed to do. I thank my brother-in-love, Alvin Wells, for covering our family as a prayerful, strong, dedicated, and loving man of God. Finally, to the still struggling addict, I pray that this work will inspire you to go a little further everyday as you walk the recovery road. PEACE, Love, and Blessings to you all.

Pastor Rachele A. Dixie, MA, MDiv

TABLE OF CONTENTS

ABOUT THE AUTHOR

Rachele A. Dixie, MA, MDiv has over 30 years of experience in mental health and addiction. She has worked in various settings including long-term residential care, inpatient groups, outpatient groups, church ministry, and community outreach. Her love and compassion for those still struggling is evident. She continues to work in the field of Pastoral Counseling. Pastor Rachele is committed to continuing to reach those who are still fighting attitudes, habits of thought, and behaviors that hinder them from moving forward in their lives.

RECOVERY DEVOTIONS FOR SPIRITUAL EMPOWERMENT

The Race Is Not Given, So Persevere

The race is not given to the swift but to those who persevere. Many of us may have heard this statement before, yet the race is never really *given* to any of us. For a person to win a race, they must work. There may be prior training, and then there is the effort it takes to walk, run, or ride in the race. Only after you have taken these necessary steps are you then declared a winner. Is this what it means to persevere? The word persevere itself means: ***to persist, to continue, to endure***. In other words, you must have some stick-to-itiveness. There is little room for sitting back and waiting for the race to come to you; you must go after it. So, in the race you are in right, now how are you persevering? Are you kicking back and not doing anything? Have you made some prior preparations to run the race? Are you running the race, walking, or just taking the ride? Depending on which one of these you are doing will determine the next steps you need to take. You are not able to declare yourself the winner, but you are able to win. ***It takes focus***. Even when you get to the finish line there are always next steps. Keep preparing, keep persevering, and keep making the right next choice. As you persevere, in the end you will receive the prize.

Weekly Questions to Ponder

What are the main thoughts that you took away from this week's devotion?

Is the focus of the devotion a true test for you in recovery?

How can you apply your personal take away from this week's devotion to your recovery this week?

What is a practice you can put into place to help you in this area?

Making a Name for Myself

Have you ever heard someone say that they want to make a name for themself? We would all like to have a name that represents who we say that we are. Some of us want status, some of us want to be known as having money, and some of us want to be known as the one in charge. The truth is ***good reputation*** comes to those who live with decency and faith. Your words have no influence if your actions do not back them up. Reputation is defined as: ***the overall quality or character as judged by people; a place in public esteem or regard.*** Do you even care what others think? There is no right or wrong answer; it is simply a personal choice. What do you think about yourself? Only you know those personal places of struggle when it comes to your own self-worth and your recovery. So far in your life what has your reputation gotten you? If your attitudes and behaviors have brought you to a point where you want change, then now is the time. Let the name you make for yourself be one that represents faith in something other than what the world sees as your status. Let your name be one that others want to call on for support, love, and wisdom. You are born to be a blessing and a forerunner for the next generation. If you are going to make a name for yourself, make it a good one. Even the richest among us do not have the best reputation. *"***A *good name* is to be chosen rather than great riches***"- Prov 22:1a*. It is the good name that makes you chosen.

Weekly Questions to Ponder

What are the main thoughts that you took away from this week's devotion?

Is the focus of the devotion a true test for you in recovery?

How can you apply your personal take away from this week's devotion to your recovery this week?

What is a practice you can put into place to help you in this area?

It's Just Paper

Have you ever been defined by what someone put on paper about you? Some of us have experienced this because perhaps we have legal offenses that are attached to our name. Or perhaps for some of us it is the infamous credit score which gives creditors the right to reject us for that home or car loan, or that apartment rental. *What is a piece of paper saying about me and does it truly reflect who I am?* Some of the kindest and most insightful people sit in jail cells because of a bad, in-the-moment choice. It is important to remember that **my identity is not found in words but in character**. Romans 5:3b-4 states: "**glory in tribulations, knowing that tribulation produces perseverance; perseverance, character; and character, hope.**" If I am representing Godly character and working toward the things that build me up and not tear me down, then it really is *just paper*. Paper definitions may offer me nothing but feelings of shame, guilt, hopelessness, and fear. The things that truly need my focus are qualities such as forgiveness, confidence, hopefulness, and serenity. You only move to the next level when you work on rebuilding you. It is in building the positive attributes that define who you are that will empower you to reach every goal that you have in sight for yourself. Do not forget, words on a page do not represent the fullness of who you are. After all, it really is just paper.

Weekly Questions to Ponder

What are the main thoughts that you took away from this week's devotion?

Is the focus of the devotion a true test for you in recovery?

How can you apply your personal take away from this week's devotion to your recovery this week?

What is a practice you can put into place to help you in this area?

This Is Not the Life

At one time or another, do you remember thinking to yourself, *This is not the life I signed up for.* You think about past mistakes, how unfair it was growing up in your family, or possibly how unfair it was growing up without a family at all. Frustration, sadness, blame, and other negative emotions come with this life. Although you may have even said things like, *I am going to make a great life for myself*, that is not the reality of your life. Thoughts may come to mind which say, *Oh please make my addiction go away. Oh, please make my debt go away. Oh, please make my fear go away. Make this go away or that go away; This is not the life I signed up for!* Nonetheless, we are still here. Still in the fight and still striving for the life we want to have. There is nothing that makes you or me exempt from life difficulties. The fact is, we did not get to sign up for our lives; we were assigned to be alive. Some of our choices may have diverted us, or some of our circumstances may not have felt fair. Yet why not try to do something different instead of looking for a way out? **Risk making a CHANGE:** make the life you want a reality and stop trying to erase your name from the sign-up sheet of life. You may not have your best life just yet, but if you keep doing what you have done it will never be the life you signed up for. Instead of rehearsing what it is not, look for the new sign-up sheet titled: ***This is Life; the best is yet to come.***

Weekly Questions to Ponder

What are the main thoughts that you took away from this week's devotion?

Is the focus of the devotion a true test for you in recovery?

How can you apply your personal take away from this week's devotion to your recovery this week?

What is a practice you can put into place to help you in this area?

Becoming Flavorful

Have you ever had a plate of food in front of you, took a bite and then realized that it needed salt? Most of us do not like to eat bland food if we can help it. We love to have some seasonings to enhance or liven up the flavor of our meal. Well, have you ever considered that you have flavor? When you walk in the room do people look at you as bland or do you bring something to the table? During your trials and storms, you are developing layers of flavor. It may seem as if what you are going through is not good but if you consider the bigger picture, you are the only one who can change the bitter into savory. Addiction does not have to make you bitter. Your story is unique, and it can salt the lives of others who may not be able to navigate their difficult situation as well as you have. Even if you think, *I am not doing a good job at this,* realize that ***you are becoming***. God is opening your flavors to become the salt that enhances your life and possibly the lives of others. Do not be discouraged by the blandness or struggle of your life right now, but allow the zest, tang, and taste to come forth to make you the right flavor for the meal that is set before you.

Weekly Questions to Ponder

What are the main thoughts that you took away from this week's devotion?

Is the focus of the devotion a true test for you in recovery?

How can you apply your personal take away from this week's devotion to your recovery this week?

What is a practice you can put into place to help you in this area?

Making a Comeback

January 3, 1993, was the wild card playoff matchup between the Houston Oilers, led by future Hall of Fame quarterback Warren Moon, and the Buffalo Bills, led by back-up Frank Reich. It was the biggest comeback game in NFL history. It was an epic game and was characterized by what was termed fandemonium. Fandemonium takes over when your team starts working their way back into the game; the cheers and the frenzy of excitement reaches its peak. We think there is no way they can lose because we are cheering them on. We have the fever, and it seems to be by sheer willpower that we, the fans in one accord with each other, spur the team back to ultimate victory. How many times have you felt like the back-up and unqualified to lead the comeback in your own life? In the comeback from addiction, we are making new efforts to win or succeed after being close to defeat or failure. Yet, defeat or failure has only been close; it does not have to be the end of our story. The way may be indirect for some of us only because sheer willpower just has not gotten us there. By ***making a new effort*** to go after all that God has for you, you must have the right attitude and mindset. It may be prayer, an attitude of gratitude, self-discipline, or gaining knowledge. Whatever it is, **YOU CAN**

MAKE A COMEBACK! If your best efforts and thinking have not worked, then try a new game plan and work with singleness of heart and mind toward your goal. As the commentators said on that day, as victory was just a few seconds away, ***It is bedlam, it is pandemonium, it is fandemonium, it is fantastic***!

Weekly Questions to Ponder

What are the main thoughts that you took away from this week's devotion?

Is the focus of the devotion a true test for you in recovery?

How can you apply your personal take away from this week's devotion to your recovery this week?

What is a practice you can put into place to help you in this area?

When You Hurt

It is hard when you experience chronic physical pain. Making a simple decision to get up to move from one room to the next can take all the emotional strength you have in that moment. As you watch other people move without hindrance from point A to point B and without wincing in pain you simply wish, *Why can't that be me?* Yet, in some ways, physical pain cannot compare to the crippling emotional pain of fighting mental illness or addiction. People do not see that you are walking with a crutch or a cane, or are in a wheelchair, yet because you have such emotional pain, sometimes you just do not feel like you can make it. How do you move forward when all you know is, "I really hurt today?" It is the power of knowing that once you stand and get your balance that eventually you will make it to the next room. No, it will not be easy and no, it will not necessarily be without pain, **BUT YOU WILL MAKE IT**. Part of the struggle is you just have to get up, do what you know you have to, and trust the process. So, stop just sitting and thinking about it, or trying to make it go away. Stop thinking the room will move to you; simply **get up**. Any hurt whether physical, emotional, spiritual, or mental does not go away because we *wish* that it would. We must take the steps to ensure that we will make it to the next room. God is faithful if you believe that he can help get you there. Sometimes we fall and many times we hurt, yet it takes a move to get to the next room. Okay, here I go…

Weekly Questions to Ponder

What are the main thoughts that you took away from this week's devotion?

Is the focus of the devotion a true test for you in recovery?

How can you apply your personal take away from this week's devotion to your recovery this week?

What is a practice you can put into place to help you in this area?

What Is the Plan Today?

Each day we wake up and may ask ourselves, *What is the plan for today?* Do I have things on my schedule that I want to do, or is it just another mindless set of things that must be accomplished? Depending on your circumstance you may be excited to engage in the day. However, for some of us, it may be another day of wondering, *How will I make it through? Will this recovery thing work today, or am I doomed to fail?* Well, you cannot have a plan without a **purpose.** Purpose (be intentional) in yourself that you will accomplish something that makes you smile or, better still, makes someone else smile today. Maybe the goal must be to think of someone else, rather than yourself. You see, if we choose to not get caught up in what we do not have and/or what we cannot do, then we are able to see more clearly. Consider the person who does not have a warm place to stay or did not have breakfast on his/her table today. Someone woke up to another 'hit' just because that is how they are surviving. The enemy *wants* us to fail, yet you can shift your mindset and say there is a great plan for this day. Why not plan to walk purposefully? Plan to love, plan to smile, plan to hope. Look in your mirror this morning and do not just ask what the plan is for today, but declare, ***GOD HAS A GREAT PLAN FOR ME TODAY!*** You just need to walk in it!

Weekly Questions to Ponder

What are the main thoughts that you took away from this week's devotion?

Is the focus of the devotion a true test for you in recovery?

How can you apply your personal take away from this week's devotion to your recovery this week?

What is a practice you can put into place to help you in this area?

Do Not Turn Off the Computer

Have you seen a message posted on the front of your computer screen which says: 'Do **not** turn off the computer?' Why is it so important to not have to go through the process of rebooting the computer after it has been turned off? With today's technology it cannot really take *that* long. However, it could be that if the computer were to be turned off, the necessary updates cannot occur, and it will take longer to boot up the next time we turn it on. Honestly, what is important here is that the computer is the electronic brain center of whatever we are using it for whether it be work, school, or pleasure. Doesn't that seem just like us always needing to be on? We either need to be ready for the next update that may come our way, or we really do not want to waste time getting started with the next agenda item on our life's 'to do' list. Well, as we journey through recovery we may occasionally need to shut down the mass of information we have stored on our hard drive. We need to delete some of the old files that are corrupting our system, and we need a reboot. If what we have been doing is overloading us, then we need to shut down and restart; we just need to make sure that our central hard drive is God. He knows exactly what viruses will affect us and are likely to crash our system. Maybe we need to download some new files and install some new programs. But if we never turn that old computer off, we will continue to get the old messages that have led us to our crash. Maybe the message we should be reading on our computer screen is '**Log all the way off to shut-down so that the GOD hardware can be installed**.'

Weekly Questions to Ponder

What are the main thoughts that you took away from this week's devotion?

Is the focus of the devotion a true test for you in recovery?

How can you apply your personal take away from this week's devotion to your recovery this week?

What is a practice you can put into place to help you in this area?

Pay Attention

Do you remember being told by a teacher or your parents, pay attention? When you heard those words, it was a wake-up call for you to focus on what was being said or taught. In your current situation are you paying attention to the right things? On this winding road of recovery, you must be careful what it is you are paying attention to. In the tough moments we can allow the negative thinking or negative emotions to capture us. We take that familiar rabbit hole and give in to what we used to do. Well, **TODAY** God is saying, ***PAY ATTENTION***; whatever you apply your mind to is the direction you will take. Prepare your mind as you enter this day to think just as a good soldier stands. ***Make your mind erect***, no swinging your arms around to grab at the old things, and for goodness' sake, keep your eyes to the front. Stay observant, stay aware, and be mindful of what you are striving after. Pay attention to God's best for you. It is out there but if you do not **PAY ATTENTION** to the right things, you might just be bound to have to repeat some difficult lessons.

Weekly Questions to Ponder

What are the main thoughts that you took away from this week's devotion?

Is the focus of the devotion a true test for you in recovery?

How can you apply your personal take away from this week's devotion to your recovery this week?

What is a practice you can put into place to help you in this area?

Hiding Behind the Mask

Sometimes people love to put on a mask. Under the mask no one can see if you have a frown or if you have a smile. They cannot tell if your face is angry or if your face is ugly. If you are beautiful you may be more at ease without a mask, but if you do not love yourself or do not think you are beautiful, you may find comfort behind the mask. In this recovery journey we may go through feelings of shame, guilt, hurt, or fear. Although we can put on a good face and say the things people want to hear, is that really moving your recovery forward? Masks take away the opportunity for transparency. They take away the opportunity for you to receive light and to give light. Once you give up the mask you may find that the power you have given to your shame, guilt, hurt, or fear does not really have any power at all. Once you allow the light onto your face maybe you will really see the beauty that God has placed in you. You will find people who understand right where you are today. Do not let a mask hinder your recovery and the bigger landscape of your life. There is beauty that you may be hiding and there is someone who needs to receive the beauty that you have. Masks disguise the true you; the true you will never shine behind the mask. Lose the mask and gain the light.

Weekly Questions to Ponder

What are the main thoughts that you took away from this week's devotion?

Is the focus of the devotion a true test for you in recovery?

How can you apply your personal take away from this week's devotion to your recovery this week?

What is a practice you can put into place to help you in this area?

The Cave of Recovery

There is a story in the Bible of the prophet Elijah who flees to a cave under fear of being killed. When He saw this, the Lord asked him "What are you doing here Elijah?" (1 Kings 19:9). This is a good question for many of us. Sometimes on this journey of recovery we want to retreat to our cave and be free from all the requirements of working our program. It seems easier to hide out and hope the feelings of distress, loneliness, or fear will go away. Yet the truth is they sit right there in the cave with you. Until you emerge, take suggestions, and listen, you will stay stuck in old emotions and thought patterns. What happens next is a lesson for each of us. In that same story Elijah goes to the mouth of the cave to listen for the voice of God. The way Elijah was used to hearing God was loud and thunderous, but in this instance, it says God was not in the wind, earthquake, or the fire; He was a still small voice (1 Kings 19:13). What are you looking for...something earth shattering and miraculous? Well, at times we just need to listen to the everyday small things that we need to do to stay on track with our recovery. We would love to have an earthquake or mighty wind come to shake it all away, but the truth is you must be willing to listen and to work. Retreating to the cave is not where you will find the tools necessary to make this recovery journey successful. You must step out of the cave and into your recovery. Only by following God's plan will you receive the victory.

Weekly Questions to Ponder

What are the main thoughts that you took away from this week's devotion?

Is the focus of the devotion a true test for you in recovery?

How can you apply your personal take away from this week's devotion to your recovery this week?

What is a practice you can put into place to help you in this area?

Grace on You

Maybe you have been one of those individuals who has heard or felt the words *Shame on you.* You have felt shame or guilt about the fact that you have an addiction that you are battling every day. Instead of supporting you, at times it feels as if people really do not get it. Shame comes much more easily than pride in the fact that you are in recovery. Let me pose this question to you: Are you walking with *shame on you*? Or with *grace on you*? Grace is defined as: ***unmerited divine assistance given to humans for their regeneration or sanctification; a virtue coming from God***. Maybe you have to see yourself as being regenerated and remade to be able to appreciate the fact that there is great *grace around you*. When we stay in our old way of thinking and accept the old labels, we will find ourselves falling back to our old behaviors. God does not want you to fall back to what you used to do, so it requires that you do not think like you used to think. No one has a right to place a label of *shame on you*, but God does have a right to place a ***veil of grace around you***. We all have shortcomings that have caused us to trip in this life. No matter what anyone says, they do not have the final judgment as to who you are. Walk in God's veil of grace and remember that you are replacing the old you with the new you. Let God be the judge of you, after all He created you. Remember there is great **GRACE UPON YOU**.

Weekly Questions to Ponder

What are the main thoughts that you took away from this week's devotion?

Is the focus of the devotion a true test for you in recovery?

How can you apply your personal take away from this week's devotion to your recovery this week?

What is a practice you can put into place to help you in this area?

The Same Old Network

You know those favorite TV shows you watch week after week? You know just what network to find them on and it becomes a mindless habit to turn to your favorite network at just the right time; the channel number seared in your memory. It does not matter if the show is an action or adventure show, a comedy, your favorite sport, or a love story. You know right when and where to tune in. At times that can be how addiction is. You tune in mindlessly to the familiar networks. You find it easy to know the exact time and location to find the people, places, and things you are familiar with. Recovery requires us to turn aside from the same old networks for a different channel. Maybe we need to upgrade our selection so that we have better options to choose from. Keeping with the same networks will put us in the same habitual mindset. I am sure you know that if you do what you always did, you will get what you always got. Is it time for you to seek out some new networks, tune into some new and more fruitful TV shows? The same networks eventually bring on the reruns that we can stare at without blinking and we still know what happens. God has a new network for you. In His network are hope, encouragement, peace, and love. Look for a better selection and find a different choice. **You never know how much more you may enjoy tuning into a new channel.**

Weekly Questions to Ponder

What are the main thoughts that you took away from this week's devotion?

Is the focus of the devotion a true test for you in recovery?

How can you apply your personal take away from this week's devotion to your recovery this week?

What is a practice you can put into place to help you in this area?

Reruns

Here is the thing about old television reruns, WE LOVE THEM! The reason we watch the reruns is we love the stories. We want to say the lines or sing the songs right along with the characters on the screen. Some of us love the old black and white television shows. Some of us, the old westerns. Some of us, the old daytime soap operas. Some of us, the old prime-time soap operas. Some of us, the old comedies. Whatever your era or whatever your genre, it is easy to be caught in the reruns. Is your battle with addiction like that? Do you find that your mind tends to get caught in the reruns that you have loved as you drive down a familiar street or hear a familiar song? It is understandable that we want to know the end of the story because when we watch reruns, we are guaranteed to know how they end. Yet, in our recovery we have to put the reruns aside and look for a new program. Our program has to be sharp, fresh, and doable. We cannot afford to make it something dull that we know every word to, and something wherein a certain ending is guaranteed. If we make our recovery about reruns, we are bound to get lazy and careless, believing, *I got this.* In this journey we must seek new associations, actions, and attitudes that will not let the rerun mentality become greater than the freshness of living this thing one day at a time. So, make sure the rerun you are enjoying is a part of the balance of your life and do not let the rerun *become* your life. It is time for your new series titled: **MY FRESH START!**

Weekly Questions to Ponder

What are the main thoughts that you took away from this week's devotion?

Is the focus of the devotion a true test for you in recovery?

How can you apply your personal take away from this week's devotion to your recovery this week?

What is a practice you can put into place to help you in this area?

Force Field

Would you love to be surrounded by a force field to protect you from every danger of mind and body? Inside the force field you would not have to be concerned about the old things that tempted you or threw you off your game. You'd be protected and never have to worry that you would fall or fail at anything. Unfortunately, this is not the reality in which we live. There is no force field around us to keep us from the things in the world that distract or upset us. Yet, there is an option for you and me when it comes to protection from distractions and temptations. God is ever present and gives us refuge. Psalms 46:1 says, ***God is our refuge and strength, A very present help in trouble.*** We can know that God truly is a force field around us if we seek after Him. The things we fill our minds with will be the things we come back to in the difficult moments. The best way to allow God to be the force field around you is to get to know Him and to know His promises. There are many ways to do that. Find a friend who you can share time with while learning about God whether through prayer, reading the Bible, or attending a church. What is the force field that you will choose? Nothing in our natural world can stop everything, but knowing a God who surrounds us with love will help us to walk through the moments that try to impede our progress toward a successful recovery. Let Him be your **FORCE FIELD**.

Weekly Questions to Ponder

What are the main thoughts that you took away from this week's devotion?

Is the focus of the devotion a true test for you in recovery?

How can you apply your personal take away from this week's devotion to your recovery this week?

What is a practice you can put into place to help you in this area?

Pressing Through the Storm

One thing I really love is a good thunderstorm. I enjoy the sound of a hard rain, the crackling sound of lightning, and a good deep boom of thunder. Many times, as a child I remember looking down our street to the west to see how dark the clouds were while anticipating if it were going to be a great thunderstorm. If my mom would let me, I loved to sit on the porch and just watch the storm. My love of thunderstorms may resonate with some of you, while others of you may hate thunderstorms. In either case the storms still come. That is much like what life can feel like in addiction. It seems to be a never-ending storm until we decide that we want something different. Just because we want to be free from having to deal with some of the stormy issues we face in life, we are not immune to the reality that this is the circumstance in which we live. Wisdom tells us that if the storm is too great, we need to find a safe location and sit still. Other situations may call for us to press through to our destination. The thing to remember is that in either case, God can take us through no matter what. He sits with us in the stillness and covers us when we must run through the rain. It is the knowing and desire to press through that God will honor. We may not have a choice about the storm coming but we do have a choice to **PRESS ON THROUGH THE STORM.**

Weekly Questions to Ponder

What are the main thoughts that you took away from this week's devotion?

Is the focus of the devotion a true test for you in recovery?

How can you apply your personal take away from this week's devotion to your recovery this week?

What is a practice you can put into place to help you in this area?

The End of the Day

What are you looking forward to when you awake in the morning? You may think about all that you want to accomplish, the people you will, or hope to, encounter, or the financial strides you will make. Yet, with all this, at times there is nothing that feels better than getting to the end of the day. You get to go to your place of safety and comfort. You get to engage with someone you love, or you simply get to sit quietly and reflect on what the day held. You may have a time of mindless TV watching or you may take time to cook a wonderful dinner. Whatever the case you are glad to have made it to the end of the day. In recovery there are days that may seem as if they will never end. At every turn you face temptation or feelings that activate those old thinking habits. You struggle to find a quiet mind or a place to let go of every disruptive emotion that is going on inside of you. You are trying to make it to the end of the day to a place where you do not feel the struggle or hear your addiction yelling at you to come back to what you used to do. The fact is you may just have to find the strategies that have helped you make it to this point and ride out the struggle. Do not get me wrong, some days will be great, and the end of the day will bring all the joys you look forward to. Other times you will see the end of the day as the rope that somebody swung over the cliff to save you. Whichever the case, know that the end of the day is coming. You can make it when you keep your eyes toward Jesus. He is there for you and He is there to support you. When you are just not sure, raise your head and look down the road. You can see it and you will make it to **THE END OF THE DAY.**

Weekly Questions to Ponder

What are the main thoughts that you took away from this week's devotion?

Is the focus of the devotion a true test for you in recovery?

How can you apply your personal take away from this week's devotion to your recovery this week?

What is a practice you can put into place to help you in this area?

Calling You Out

Have you ever had someone call you out on your crap and you were seriously offended? We think about the person and wonder, *What gives them the right to think they can say that to me?* Maybe it is that they have been through some of the same things you have been through or perhaps they know you or love you enough to think that you just might be willing to hear the truth about yourself from them. Sometimes our go to is that they need to take their own inventory before they think they can take ours. Well, let me propose to you that you take time to examine yourself. 2 Corinthians 13:5 says, "***Examine yourselves to see whether you are living in the faith. Test yourselves. Do you not realize that Jesus Christ is in you?—unless, indeed, you fail to meet the test!"*** Are you living out this walk or are you failing to meet the test because you refuse to examine what someone might be calling you out on? Now do not get me wrong, we do not have to take corrections from everyone. However, maybe we ought to evaluate the vessel through whom God is speaking. Even better than that, why do we not take the time to examine ourselves daily to see if we are truly walking in faith or simply taking for granted another day God has blessed us to see? Take to heart that Jesus Christ is in you and He wants the best for His vessel. Anytime we think we cannot be called to correction we are in error. If we want to get to the place where we can be confident in our actions, then we must examine ourselves daily. The fact is sometimes it is God who is **CALLING YOU OUT** because He wants to bring out something better in you.

Weekly Questions to Ponder

What are the main thoughts that you took away from this week's devotion?

Is the focus of the devotion a true test for you in recovery?

How can you apply your personal take away from this week's devotion to your recovery this week?

What is a practice you can put into place to help you in this area?

Justifiably Frustrated

Look, I know that getting through this addiction thing is hard; in fact, at times, it feels seriously unfair. You go through the days asking the Lord, "Why me?" Or saying, "Really? This is what my life is right now?!" In those moments you feel as if you truly need God to hear you and change your situation. However, reality hits you and the situation does not change. You are justifiably frustrated. You feel hurt, angry, and abandoned by family and by God. The truth is God has not abandoned you, but He is trying to get you where He wants you to be. You are becoming...becoming a warrior, becoming a voice, becoming an example of perseverance that will cause you to meet the purpose that God has for you. Still, you are justifiably frustrated. Nonetheless, do not let the situation you may have put yourself in or that God has allowed, turn you from your goal. Stay the course and see the road. As you continue to press past the frustration God will bring you into focus. You are positioned to succeed in this endeavor of sobriety. Do not let your frustration win but know that as you focus you may find that you were frustrated but the result did justify your frustration. Sometimes it is the end that justifies the means. Hmmm, pause and calmly think of that.

Weekly Questions to Ponder

What are the main thoughts that you took away from this week's devotion?

Is the focus of the devotion a true test for you in recovery?

How can you apply your personal take away from this week's devotion to your recovery this week?

What is a practice you can put into place to help you in this area?

What Does It Mean to Be Made?

I thought this was a good question to begin the day. What does it mean to be made? There is a Bible verse which says: **I will praise You, for I am fearfully *and* wonderfully made (Psalm 139:14a).** Many times after feeling the burden of shame or guilt due to our addiction, as we work to regain our footing in society it is hard for us to believe that God has made us wonderfully. We believe we really are too messed up for God to even care about. Yet, part of the definition of *made* says this: the right qualities *to be* or *to do* something. When God made you, He placed quality in you; the right qualities to do and to become who you were intended to be. In this recovery journey what qualities does it take to be wonderfully made? It is in these moments of exploration when we must put aside the negative and push ourselves toward the positive attributes which we hold. To be made we must organize our plan, engage in the task necessary, and put together the right ingredients to ensure that today we are **being made** into the person we desire to be. Do not simply take as cliché that God does not make mistakes. You are certainly no mistake but please give yourself space to allow God to continue to make you into His image. Addiction is not the final answer to who we were made to be; it is only a challenge to derail the true character of God in us. Remember God is the ultimate creator and we, mankind, are His greatest creation. You are truly fearfully and **WONDERFULLY made**.

Weekly Questions to Ponder

What are the main thoughts that you took away from this week's devotion?

Is the focus of the devotion a true test for you in recovery?

How can you apply your personal take away from this week's devotion to your recovery this week?

What is a practice you can put into place to help you in this area?

Release

Have you ever felt physically, emotionally, or spiritually restrained for some reason? That feeling of being confined physically, emotionally, or spiritually can be so daunting that it is hard to think your way through. You may not see the way out or, in the addicted mind, you may believe you need that thing you are addicted to so that you can feel free. Gaining relief or release from the burdens or the oppressive thoughts and emotions that come with addiction is part of this recovery story. Recovery is giving yourself over to a process that will, on some level, allow you to give yourself permission to release the weights. Every release does not look the same. For some it may be a course of counseling, for others support groups, and yet for others the intensity of an inpatient program. With all these methods the primary release comes through an understanding of the forgiveness we receive through Jesus Christ. With many in recovery the hardest task is to forgive yourself and one of the greatest worries is that others will not forgive you. Nonetheless, it is a relationship with Christ that will change your trajectory. To release everything, you have held or that has held you back brings great victory. You are no longer confined to the addiction story of your life, but you are released to the story God has for your life. Take these thoughts from Matthew 6:34 (MSG) **"Give your entire attention to what God is doing right now, and don't get worked up about what may or may not happen tomorrow. God will help you deal with whatever hard things come up when the time comes."** In other words, you can RELEASE IT!

Weekly Questions to Ponder

What are the main thoughts that you took away from this week's devotion?

Is the focus of the devotion a true test for you in recovery?

How can you apply your personal take away from this week's devotion to your recovery this week?

What is a practice you can put into place to help you in this area?

Is It Time to Go?

Each of us at one time or another has had to prepare ourselves whether physically or emotionally, to go. It may be to go to the workplace, out to dinner with a friend, a doctor's appointment, or any of the other 10,000 places we have to go to in this life. Essentially, we must move out or away from the place where we are and get to the place where we want to be. That is what GO is all about. It is **to take a certain course or follow a certain procedure.** This journey that you are on may have certain rules applied to it and certainly one of the requirements is that there is no option for standing still. In recovery there is a course you can take, a course that has been proven to be successful for many. Meetings, sponsorship, and a relationship with the God of your understanding all hold a means to success. Nonetheless, it is still very necessary that you move. Your course may have some different types of twists and turns than others, but make no mistake, your course must move forward. Do not let going backward or standing still become an option for you. When you are dressed and are prepped it is time to go. Have you been in preparation? Are your clothes on? Is your make-up ready? Is your cologne sprayed on? Whatever your routine for *going*, it sounds like you are ready. **NOW, IT IS TIME TO GO!!**

Weekly Questions to Ponder

What are the main thoughts that you took away from this week's devotion?

Is the focus of the devotion a true test for you in recovery?

How can you apply your personal take away from this week's devotion to your recovery this week?

What is a practice you can put into place to help you in this area?

Lip Service Is Useless

If you have gone through the programs of recovery just to find yourself back at the same point down the road, you may feel that things will never change. Oftentimes people can learn the language and culture of recovery without ever having found the lightbulb that turns on how they can become successful at staying clean. At some point recovery must become a part of you. It must be ingested into your very being as a lifeline. The jargon or going through the motions never hurts the people who are around you; it only hurts you. When you begin to believe your own lip service you make your recovery a useless play that can have a tragic ending. You see, lip service is useless. We can form our mouths to say anything, but the Bible says in 1 Corinthians 2:11a: **For what man knows the things of a man except the spirit of the man which is in him?** Basically, each of us knows whether we are being honest or not and no one else can really tell one way or another. If you invest in your recovery you will find that it is not *what* you are saying that matters; but it is what you are doing that is key. Are you being real with yourself? Or, are you most concerned with sounding good to everyone else so that they think you are getting better? That may work for a while but eventually it will all come out. So, decide to not just talk about it, but to be about it. Be about doing recovery for your own good. Remember this is important for your life and at the end of the day **LIP SERVICE IS STILL USELESS**.

Weekly Questions to Ponder

What are the main thoughts that you took away from this week's devotion?

Is the focus of the devotion a true test for you in recovery?

How can you apply your personal take away from this week's devotion to your recovery this week?

What is a practice you can put into place to help you in this area?

I'm in a Mood

Sometimes you wake up and you are just in a mood. Not certain if you are sad, mad, mellow, lazy, or just blah. This can be one of the most difficult days for your recovery. All you know is you want to feel something and what you are used to doing is what you are trying not to do. In these moments you may find yourself pulling on every recovery strategy and tool that you know. Do I call someone? Do I go to a meeting? Do I work a step? Or, do I just try to push my way through? Well, this is the perfect time to give God a try. If you are new in your faith you might just take some time to have a quiet and honest conversation with God. No fancy words are required, just let Him know how you feel and that it is frustrating to feel this way without using. Trust me, God will understand, and your honesty will provide a release for you. If you are a person who has a deeper relationship with God, it might just be time for you to get back to your study of God's Word. Just as Jesus' disciples asked in **Luke 17:5, *Lord, "Increase our faith!"*** we cannot expect to grow in faith without continuing to get to know the God we say we believe. So instead of being stuck and feeling sorry for yourself because you are **'in a mood'** make a move toward God; you can be assured He will move toward you. Do not let a mood cause you to lose sight of the bigger picture. It is just one day in a lifetime of moods. You never know about tomorrow; ***JOY is coming in the morning***.

Weekly Questions to Ponder

What are the main thoughts that you took away from this week's devotion?

Is the focus of the devotion a true test for you in recovery?

How can you apply your personal take away from this week's devotion to your recovery this week?

What is a practice you can put into place to help you in this area?

Authority

All of us at some point in our life have had to submit to authority. We have been under the command of another; whether a parent, a boss, or governmental systems. That is one kind of authority and then there is another type where you may hear people say that someone is an *authority* on a matter. Well, which type of authority is necessary in this recovery process? In this journey, one of the first things we must surrender to is the fact that we are powerless to our addiction. We make a conscious decision to turn our will and turn our life over to a Power greater than ourselves. In essence, we give authority of our lives to this Power that we deem wise enough to help us through. We allow the influences of spirituality, support groups, sponsorship, and more to be in command of our decisions, realizing that our past choices have not rendered a good outcome to our lives. As we continue in this process we prayerfully move to a place where we have a testimony as to the effectiveness of recovery. We, on some levels, become an authority on recovery. Yet, could this be a danger zone for many of us in our daily walk? We have given ourselves the title of being an authority on the matter when we still need to come under the authority to the process. Since it is a process, as life itself is, we do not want to put ourselves on a pedestal that would cause us not to remain intentional about our journey. We still need to submit to the influence, thought, opinion, and command of our recovery program. Ultimately, you can call it whatever you like but God is the supreme authority for each one of us. We must allow His expertise to influence our decisions to live out a successful recovery journey. So, do not be angry that you must come under authority, simply KNOW: **GOD IS the authority on ALL matters concerning sobriety and life.**

Weekly Questions to Ponder

What are the main thoughts that you took away from this week's devotion?

Is the focus of the devotion a true test for you in recovery?

How can you apply your personal take away from this week's devotion to your recovery this week?

What is a practice you can put into place to help you in this area?

Take Suggestions

In our world today there is a mantra that seems to overtake many of the decisions we make. That mantra is, "I know what is best for me." It appears that several have taken this mindset as a way out, a way out of confronting their feelings, and even in some cases, confronting their fears. My question to the individual who is still recovering who may be reading this is, *Has your best thinking gotten you here?* In the circles of recovery, you may have heard this statement on more than one occasion. You may have said it aloud to yourself or to someone else. Whether you are fresh in your recovery journey or have been doing it for a while, this is not the time to stop taking suggestions. Certainly, we understand where we are in the process, yet becoming an independent operator in a program where support is a key component can be detrimental. Questioning yourself as to what you are feeling or what you may be afraid of can be a big step in allowing suggestions in your life. Taking a suggestion does not cause any risk to you. You may feel like you do not want to do it or that the person does not know what he/she is talking about; however, at the end of the day remember it was your best thinking that got you here. If you want to improve the thinking that got you here, learn that it is okay to **take suggestions.**

Weekly Questions to Ponder

What are the main thoughts that you took away from this week's devotion?

Is the focus of the devotion a true test for you in recovery?

How can you apply your personal take away from this week's devotion to your recovery this week?

What is a practice you can put into place to help you in this area?

No One Believes Me

Don't you hate it when people do not believe you? You can be doing all the right things for your recovery. You are going to meetings, working with your sponsor, working the steps, building your relationship with your Higher Power, yet they still do not believe you. Based on your past, people have decided you will not change and that you will not be able to stay clean. How frustrating is that?! When you work hard to be successful in the program you feel you deserve to be believed. Well, welcome to the club! Oftentimes, you can do everything according to the program and according to your personal desire to conquer your addiction. Nevertheless, the proof only comes out over time. The saying, "I can show you better than I can tell you," is where you must land. You must stay secure in the truth of what you are accomplishing. In fact, in the Bible the Pharisees constantly came against Jesus and did not believe He was the One who was to come; he was the Christ. He was often not believed even as he performed miracles, taught the multitudes, and lived a life of ministry. So why get discouraged because people do not believe you? God is the one who knows the truth. If you are not being truthful, you should not be believed; but if you are, what others think doesn't matter. Stand up and show the evidence that YOU CAN BE BELIEVED and. Remember **sometimes you must SHOW it, then you can tell it**.

Weekly Questions to Ponder

What are the main thoughts that you took away from this week's devotion?

Is the focus of the devotion a true test for you in recovery?

How can you apply your personal take away from this week's devotion to your recovery this week?

What is a practice you can put into place to help you in this area?

Pause Today

During our lives, we try our best to plan out what our day or our week may look like. We get our phones out to check the calendar for that next appointment and hope we did not plan something that conflicts with our daily to do list. Some days we feel as if we are hitting on all cylinders. The calendar runs smoothly and all that needs to be accomplished is done. But what about those days that get off course? We found that we booked too many things in a limited amount of time and one meeting ran over into the next. We become frustrated and are thrown off our game. Things are just not working out and our irritation with everything has spilled over. This is the moment we must take a PAUSE. *Pause means a temporary stop in whatever action you are engaged with.* Sometimes that action is mental rather than physical. Thoughts can begin to race, and we become overwhelmed because our day is not working out as planned. For people in recovery, it can feel dangerous to not have something to do each moment. Secretly you worry if you will be tempted to go back to what you used to do. Do you have to go back? Absolutely not! Romans 12:2 puts it this way: "***And be not conformed to this world: but be ye transformed by the renewing of your mind, that ye may prove what is that***

good, and acceptable, and perfect, will of God." You have the power to PAUSE; the power to renew your mind. In doing so, you can prove that the day does not control you, but you control the day.

Weekly Questions to Ponder

What are the main thoughts that you took away from this week's devotion?

Is the focus of the devotion a true test for you in recovery?

How can you apply your personal take away from this week's devotion to your recovery this week?

What is a practice you can put into place to help you in this area?

Something on My Mind

When the heaviness of life starts to come at you it seems as if it comes all at once. It is hard to get a clear thought because you feel you need to figure out every situation right now without giving yourself time to breathe. When things are on our mind, we can become irrational and unable to take each situation as it comes, planning for one thing at a time. When in recovery you must be aware that your automatic reflex is to do what makes you feel numb. Getting the high from your drug, alcohol, gambling, sex, food, or whatever you struggle with is the easiest way out of dealing with what is on your mind. When others ask you how you are doing and your response is, "I*t's nothing, I just have something on my mind,*" that is a quick way to open the door to a relapse. You have to be willing to open up to someone about all the things which may be on your mind. Sometimes you need that rational objective voice to help you sort through all the noise in your head. Taking things one situation at a time, one day at a time, and even one moment at a time is how you make it through without going back to the automatic reflex. God places people in our circle so that we do not have to traverse the challenges alone. Use what God has placed right in front of you so that you can clear your mind.

Remember there is greater for you because the Bible says: **"We have the mind of Christ" (1 Corinthians 2:16b).** What mind is that? One that is humble and submissive in the knowledge that God the Father has a plan and has ALL things well in hand.

Weekly Questions to Ponder

What are the main thoughts that you took away from this week's devotion?

Is the focus of the devotion a true test for you in recovery?

How can you apply your personal take away from this week's devotion to your recovery this week?

What is a practice you can put into place to help you in this area?

Inside Out

One of the things that can happen when we wash our clothes is that they can get turned inside out as they go through the cycle of washing and then drying.. As we are folding or hanging up those items that have been turned inside out, we have to take an extra second or two to turn them right-side out. As you work on yourself in this recovery journey there may be times when you feel you are working from the inside out. All those internal conflicts that come with changing thoughts and behaviors that have been so familiar seem to come one right after the other. You get one area turned right-side out, then here comes the next thing. Maybe not feeling so frustrated when these things arise will require that you change your perspective from the inside out. Instead of looking at fixing yourself (or the laundry) as something that is going to take a few extra seconds, why not see it as something that will help you look better? When you finally put that shirt or those pants on, they are going to look so much better because you took the extra few seconds to turn them right-side out. Don't you think *you* are worth some extra time if a piece of laundry is? You will see as you go through the process that being right-side out was always there for you. You, however, are the one who must take the time to make sure it shows. Turning your situation around is absolutely possible; turn it over to God and remember, "**With men this is impossible; but with God all things are possible.**" (Matthew 19:26b)

Weekly Questions to Ponder

What are the main thoughts that you took away from this week's devotion?

Is the focus of the devotion a true test for you in recovery?

How can you apply your personal take away from this week's devotion to your recovery this week?

What is a practice you can put into place to help you in this area?

In the Present

When you are trying to work a sound recovery plan one of the things you must think about is staying in the present. It is easy to get consumed with everything in your life that is wrong. On the other hand, it may be that there is not enough to do and you are overtaken by your own boredom. In either case, our thoughts can very quickly spin down the rabbit hole. We can find every reason to pick up right where we left off in our addiction. By remaining in the present, which simply means "staying in the now or something in progress," we can better consider the fallout of any course of action we choose to take. In Romans 8:18 the Bible says, "**I consider that the sufferings of this present time are not worth comparing with the glory about to be revealed to us.**" By allowing God to be present with us in the moments of challenge we can press our way through to a better outcome, to a greater revelation of His glory for us. Trying to rush ahead of God or fall back to our old behaviors may cause us to miss the blessing. In the midst of addiction you have missed enough. Just stay in the present and soak in the good that God has for you. It is okay not to know all the answers right now but what you can know is that God is present with you; let Him reveal ***His best***. One day at a time, one moment at a time, just stay IN THE PRESENT and see what God will do. You will gain strength for your present which you did not even know that you had.

Weekly Questions to Ponder

What are the main thoughts that you took away from this week's devotion?

Is the focus of the devotion a true test for you in recovery?

How can you apply your personal take away from this week's devotion to your recovery this week?

What is a practice you can put into place to help you in this area?

Mind Your Mind

Our mind is a powerful tool, a tool which can be used to move us toward the direction and purpose God has for our lives. It is in the times that we become slack in how we think or what we allow into our minds that we can turn to all the wrong things. Part of the process of recovery is that we must change our thinking behaviors. When we do not change our thinking, we will have the same responses to situations that we have used for years. Some of you may have heard the saying, *Who is minding the store?* Well, consider your mind as a store that needs maintaining in every area. In the same way you are willing to take the necessary steps to take care of the store, its inventory, and its cleanliness, you ought to be willing to take the steps to **mind your mind**. We can certainly be careful about what we ingest into our spirits. The things we watch and the things we listen to all influence how we think. If you want to keep a clearer mind you may get into habits such as meditation or prayer. Let your conversations speak of positive things and not negative. Let the people you engage with have similar goal sets to yours. In the Bible, the book of Amos 3:3 it says: "**Can two walk together, unless they are agreed?**" When you speak of agreement you have to line up thoughts with behaviors. In recovery this is key to you taking that next step. As you continue in the journey you become better at the awareness needed to maintain a good thought life. In whatever we do, each one of us needs to get into the practice of MINDING OUR MIND. When we do this, we will see our minds and our behaviors become the good things which we are striving toward.

Weekly Questions to Ponder

What are the main thoughts that you took away from this week's devotion?

Is the focus of the devotion a true test for you in recovery?

How can you apply your personal take away from this week's devotion to your recovery this week?

What is a practice you can put into place to help you in this area?

Poor Visibility

Each of us could probably think of a time when we were driving, or possibly even walking along, and experienced poor visibility. The snow, rain, or maybe even fog began to make it hard to see even inches in front of us. When you experience a visibility problem the temptation is to stop and hope it passes quickly. Yet, the torrential downpour of the rain, the settling of the fog, or the heavy snowfall does not always go away when we would like it too. This can very well be like the days in recovery that seem most difficult. You would love to not have the intrusive thoughts or experience the sights or the sounds which may trigger thoughts of use. Sometimes we must press our way through when the visibility is poor. When we are feeling the uncertainty of what recovery can bring, we must believe in what will happen when it clears up. There are tough days and moments, yet when the visibility is better you are much more able to maneuver your way through. Poor visibility is not something that lasts forever but if you stop you may have to wait longer than is necessary to get to your destination. Press your way through and believe that things will clear up. It takes faith to keep going sometimes but remember as it says in 2 Corinthians 5:7 ***"For we walk by faith, not by sight."*** Have faith that pressing through the storm is worth it even when you experience poor visibility.

Weekly Questions to Ponder

What are the main thoughts that you took away from this week's devotion?

Is the focus of the devotion a true test for you in recovery?

How can you apply your personal take away from this week's devotion to your recovery this week?

What is a practice you can put into place to help you in this area?

Seasons

Some people love the change of seasons. Depending on where you were raised or where you presently live, you may enjoy seeing creation transform from one season to the next. There are those who are cold weather fans and love to see the snowfall and feel the chill in the air. Others want to experience that 90-degree heat and as much sunshine as possible. Yet, it is those in-between seasons that can be most beautiful. As the trees begin to bud and the landscape of the grass changes from brown to green, there can be a refreshing change that comes with spring. Oh, but the fall brings the change of leaves as the colors pop with bright red, orange, and yellow hues. This is when people may genuinely appreciate the beauty of nature and creation. No matter what your preference, it is certain that the change of seasons should come. Much like nature, our lives hold seasons. As you move away from your old lifestyle and habits, you are transforming and creating new habits in your life. Your winter season is coming to an end, and you are beginning to experience the fresh green landscape of spring. New growth takes place and, with the right watering, the seeds that have been planted begin to flower into beautiful new life. It is exciting to consider the seasons of our lives changing. We do not have to stay in the same place but we can experience the newness that is happening. Isaiah 43:19a puts it this way: "***Behold, I will do a new thing, Now, it shall spring forth; Shall you not know it?***" Are you ready for your new season?

Weekly Questions to Ponder

What are the main thoughts that you took away from this week's devotion?

Is the focus of the devotion a true test for you in recovery?

How can you apply your personal take away from this week's devotion to your recovery this week?

What is a practice you can put into place to help you in this area?

Investment

How many of you have ever made an investment in stocks, a particular product, or a company? We may have looked at our investments as a way to gain security and become financially sound. Yet, what happens if our investment falls through? Putting all our eggs in one basket could be dangerous so it is probably wise to invest in more than one place. Nevertheless, with all of this, the primary investment we must make is in ourselves. In recovery it is important to not take your investment lightly but to research and continue to seek out what is working in your process. When we invest it means we are committing (money) in order to earn a financial return. This is defined in monetary terminology but what is key is the fact that we must **commit**. Recovery requires commitment. Through our committing we will gain a return on our very life. We can use this as a chance to regain relationships, change our thinking, and increase the benefits that come with a sober future. One thing you must buy into in this process is that you are worth the investment. The past does not define where you can go when you put your commitment in the right areas. Paul shares this in Ephesians 4:1 "I therefore, the prisoner in the Lord, beg you to **lead a life worthy of the calling** to which you have been called." He implores the Ephesians to live up to the purpose for which God had for them. You, too, are worth the investment because there is a call in you; look for every opportunity to invest in you.

Weekly Questions to Ponder

What are the main thoughts that you took away from this week's devotion?

Is the focus of the devotion a true test for you in recovery?

How can you apply your personal take away from this week's devotion to your recovery this week?

What is a practice you can put into place to help you in this area?

The Price Is Right

How many of you have ever watched the game show *The Price is Right*? It is one of my favorites. Watching contestants anticipate the possibility of having their name called as the announcer invites them to "Come on down" to Contestants' Row causes high excitement. Jumping and shouting come with the overflow of emotion when it is their own name that they hear knowing that they actually may be coming on stage to win the big prize, and maybe even the showcase. We would all love it if we could win the prize of our dreams, possibly a vacation or a new car. Why not think of your life as a prize? When you consider all that you have been through, are you not worth the work of living your life as a prize? Philippians 3:13b-14 shares: "***forgetting what lies behind and straining forward to what lies ahead, I press on toward the goal for the prize of the heavenly call of God in Christ Jesus."*** All that has happened in the past does not compare to where your life can take you now. Consider the price you have paid for your past? Is your recovery too high of a price to gain back things lost and move toward a heavenly calling? As you continue your journey, place the proper value and worth on the time you put into the prized you. The past is the past and does not need to be repeated.

Remember, a new life is in your sights. You are the showcase and it all can be yours if...THE PRICE IS RIGHT!

Weekly Questions to Ponder

What are the main thoughts that you took away from this week's devotion?

Is the focus of the devotion a true test for you in recovery?

How can you apply your personal take away from this week's devotion to your recovery this week?

What is a practice you can put into place to help you in this area?

Moving the Mountain

Does your situation ever feel like an immovable mountain? You want to see your life move to the next chapter, but you continue to feel the mountains pressing up against you on every side. It could be a legal situation, not having that job you need to make ends meet, or a bad relationship that keeps coming back around. Why won't that mountain move? The question nags at you. *What am I doing wrong?* The truth is, you have the power in you to move the mountain, but the power is not activated. The way you think and the things you speak are both avenues to being able to move the mountain that you want moved. Jesus says in Matthew 17:20: **"I say to you, if you have faith as a mustard seed, you will say to this mountain, 'Move from here to there,' and it will move; *and nothing will be impossible for you.*"** Recovery is not an impossible journey, but it is a tough one. The question is whether or not you put in the work or if you are looking for someone else to move your mountain. It takes a mustard seed of faith. Faith requires a changed mindset and an investment in time with God. While walking your recovery journey know that better days are ahead of you. Know that you can speak to the mountains whether spiritual, emotional, or physical because Jesus says, IT WILL

MOVE. Are you in the mountain moving business today? All it takes is that mustard seed of faith.

Weekly Questions to Ponder

What are the main thoughts that you took away from this week's devotion?

Is the focus of the devotion a true test for you in recovery?

How can you apply your personal take away from this week's devotion to your recovery this week?

What is a practice you can put into place to help you in this area?

Dangers in the Wilderness

At times we can feel as if we are going through a wilderness experience. We are in that place where there appears to be no good direction to go. We can experience thoughts that cause us to condemn ourselves because of past mistakes. We may feel faithful at one moment and then doubtful the next. Standing in the middle of a barren spiritual place can be difficult. It can cause you to want to give up and go back to those people, places, or things which are familiar. Instead of giving God a chance to place a new path before you, you just let every negative thing have its way and you are stuck. Those are the dangers in the wilderness, but the other side is the opportunity to change in the wilderness. It is in the wilderness where you do not have to be swayed by other human voices and you have an opportunity to truly hear from God. The wilderness is defined as: *a tract or region* ***uninhabited by human beings;*** *An area essentially* ***undisturbed by human activity.*** This is the very place where you can shut down the noise and learn to hear the voice of God for your life. On the other side of your wilderness journey God can give you peace on the path He has for you. Psalms 29:11 shares: "**The Lord will give strength to His people; The Lord will bless His people with *peace*.** Your wilderness place is not to harm you, but to strengthen you while you walk it out with the Lord. Do not fall for the dangers of the wilderness but shift your perspective to see the good path that God has laid for you on the other side of it.

Weekly Questions to Ponder

What are the main thoughts that you took away from this week's devotion?

Is the focus of the devotion a true test for you in recovery?

How can you apply your personal take away from this week's devotion to your recovery this week?

What is a practice you can put into place to help you in this area?

Keeping Balance

There are so many areas of our lives that we must keep hold of that at times it may feel difficult to balance it all. If you have ever been on a pair of roller skates or ice skates, or can think back to when you first learned to ride a bike, you had to work at keeping your balance. Oftentimes, that work included many falls. You may have gotten up feeling sore, but if you want the enjoyment of the activity you got up and kept going. Some of the things that we work at balancing are our home lives, work lives, and social lives, our finances, physical health, and eating right; the list goes on and on. All of this is more challenging when coupled with the fact that you now must work on keeping a sound recovery program in place. Frankly however, it is not that you have to sacrifice one for the other. Good recovery offers you the opportunity to bring things together in a way that will benefit the entirety of your life. When you are at home by yourself you can balance the challenges of good health, socialization, and so on. The Bible tells us in Romans 8:28 that "***all things work together for good*** *to those who love God, to those who are the called according to His purpose.*" The *things* can be numerous but when you work together with God for your life, it certainly will turn out for the good. Keeping balance does not have to be burdensome. It does, however, require your focus and attention. Remember *all* means *all,* so allow God to work all things to your good. Allow for the good, the bad, and the ugly to reach the purpose God has planned for you.

Weekly Questions to Ponder

What are the main thoughts that you took away from this week's devotion?

Is the focus of the devotion a true test for you in recovery?

How can you apply your personal take away from this week's devotion to your recovery this week?

What is a practice you can put into place to help you in this area?

Stuck

Quite often you can hear someone use the phrase "I feel stuck." They may feel stuck regarding a job, a relationship, their recovery, or at that moment they may even feel stuck in life overall Feeling stuck is no way to gain good footing in relation to your recovery. It is important to evaluate the things that are making you feel stuck and what your role is in it. Are you stuck because of complacency, procrastination, or continually making bad decisions? Have you gone back to old mindsets and behavior patterns that are not propelling you forward to the next thing God has for you? In this life of recovery, the main thing you must get is honesty because you are meant to step into a new season for your life. Those relationships or attitudes that have gotten you to this stuck place are going to take work to change. You do not get to give a minimal effort and then expect a maximum result. Consider some of the things that are happening to you and around you. God may be not trying to simply get your attention, but He may be asking you to give more of an effort. You see the thing is, with God you are never stuck. He is always moving you forward although you may not like the way that he's doing it. Your job is to put your all into the process. Stop procrastinating, living complacently, or making the same old choices that give you the same old results. Sacrifice what *you* want for what *God* wants for you. Move from being stuck to being free. When we give it to Jesus he says: "**So if the Son makes you free, you will be free indeed**" – Jn 8:36. Do not stay in the stuck place, there is nothing there anymore. Trust that living free is God's best for you!

Weekly Questions to Ponder

What are the main thoughts that you took away from this week's devotion?

Is the focus of the devotion a true test for you in recovery?

How can you apply your personal take away from this week's devotion to your recovery this week?

What is a practice you can put into place to help you in this area?

HOW

Honesty, open-mindedness, and willingness are three concepts which can be the difference between recovery success and recovery disaster. When people ask how you do this or that, they are seeking a practical way to handle whatever situation needs to be addressed. Well, the practical things to consider in recovery reside in these ideas. If you cannot be honest, how will you begin to break the cycles that have kept you in the dark places of your addiction? By its very nature addiction carries an overtone of secrecy so it requires the change to transparency that being honest brings. **Job 31:6** puts it this way: "**Let me be weighed on *honest* scales, That God may know my integrity**." So, what about those thoughts you have boxed in that cause you to justify why you continue to use? It is being open-minded that will allow you to expand your thoughts and move into a life wherein you do not fall back into your addiction as a solution. Willingness says, *I will make the effort to change*. It is the unwilling soul that continues on the dark path of addiction. What is your *how* today? Are you going to make yourself accountable to the HOW of recovery or are you going to give yourself over to the bondage of addiction? When we put work into these concepts it will begin to open us to the thinking patterns of change which can move us forward. Only you know your level of HOW, but so does God. Let Him help you make the changes that give you a practical path to becoming free from your addiction.

Weekly Questions to Ponder

What are the main thoughts that you took away from this week's devotion?

Is the focus of the devotion a true test for you in recovery?

How can you apply your personal take away from this week's devotion to your recovery this week?

What is a practice you can put into place to help you in this area?

Transformer

Who would not love to be like the Transformers in the famous movie series? It would be wonderful if we could readjust ourselves from trucks or cars, into great fighting machines, and then back to the trucks or cars to get us to where we need to go. That may seem like a lot to think about or work toward. However, as a person who has battled addiction, it is now time to become the transformer and work on changing to the appearance that will help you fight the battle before you. As you become stronger you will be more secure in knowing when you will need to rise from your simplest form to your greatest form. It is through the power at work in you that you can lay aside what may be thought of as weakness to become a great force that can alter the situation. Let God be that power that operates to transform you. In John 1:12 it says, "**But as many as received Him, to them He gave power to become the sons of God, even to them that believe on his name.**" You are His son or daughter. As you grow in spiritual stature it is your belief in what God is doing and has done which will bring you the power to change. Live a life that does not only shift in its outward appearance, but from the inside as well. The transformer car always had its strength inside, but when the time came to fight the enemy, he had to **POWER** up. Are you a transformer? Believe that recovery is on the inside of you and transform **TODAY.** Let the battle begin!!

Weekly Questions to Ponder

What are the main thoughts that you took away from this week's devotion?

Is the focus of the devotion a true test for you in recovery?

How can you apply your personal take away from this week's devotion to your recovery this week?

What is a practice you can put into place to help you in this area?

Meanwhile

Not sure how many of you remember the old show *Hee Haw* (I am probably dating myself), but they had a great way of taking you back to a skit that seemingly kept moving while you watched what was happening on your screen. The phrase they used was, "Meanwhile back at the ranch." I always enjoyed seeing what had happened while we were away. Did the story move in the direction that I thought it might, or was there an interesting twist? That is sometimes how recovery can be. You are in the process of doing the work and the lives of the people around appear to be moving on smoothly, but *meanwhile back at the ranch,* you may be struggling. You have had some hard days and the moments do not seem to be making sense. Yet, things are still moving. Just like the ranch the story will continue to move even when we do not see it, let God continue to move your story forward. It may not look as if things are progressing, but they are. You are developing the narrative of your life as God works things for your good behind the scenes. The spectator loves to see the story unfold but the truth is sometimes it is ugly behind the scenes. There are mix-ups with the set or messed-up lines by the actors. However, this is not a skit, it is your life. You must be invested in making it turn out with a positive ending for you. So as life goes forward there are a lot of storylines we may see on your screen, but **meanwhile** take charge of the backdrop. There may be some interesting twists but your narrative at the ranch is between you and God, so make it a good one.

Weekly Questions to Ponder

What are the main thoughts that you took away from this week's devotion?

Is the focus of the devotion a true test for you in recovery?

How can you apply your personal take away from this week's devotion to your recovery this week?

What is a practice you can put into place to help you in this area?

Old Garbage

Most of us have had to take the garbage out at some point in our life. Whether your parents assigned it as a chore, or you are taking care of your own home, taking the garbage out is a requirement. This is a task we may not enjoy, but we might feel worse if we let it remain. Bad smells, insects, or even worse rodents, would invade our living area. Rotting garbage is definitely not something we want to deal with. Recovery is a process which insists that we get rid of some of the garbage that is in our lives. We must dispose of old habits, thinking patterns, attitudes, and people who will stink up our lives if we do not make some changes. This is the case for anyone who desires to live a life of faith. God will require that we put out the garbage that keeps us in danger of being infested. The question is, how do we begin to produce a clean vessel? It begins with an honest confession of our areas of weakness. When we are open enough to give over to God the parts of our lives we need help in, He will help us. A familiar scripture in **Psalms 51:10** says this: "**Create in me a clean heart, O God, And renew a right spirit within me.**" God can make what is wrong with us right. He is the one who has the power to help us get the freshening we need to make a fresh start. By removing some of the garbage out of our lives we can change our aroma. It is called acceptance. Accept that taking out the garbage is one chore that is not optional. Remember to take out the garbage TODAY so as not to let it rot; you will be glad that you did.

Weekly Questions to Ponder

What are the main thoughts that you took away from this week's devotion?

Is the focus of the devotion a true test for you in recovery?

How can you apply your personal take away from this week's devotion to your recovery this week?

What is a practice you can put into place to help you in this area?

Words Matter

In this journey of life all of us, at one time or another, have experienced someone saying to us words that hurt. The fact that you may have been in this situation can cause you to feel like you are less important or that people really do not care. As a part of being in recovery no one is asking you to become immune to your feelings. You have to consider who you are becoming and take careful consideration of the words which have hurt you in the past. The danger to you as a recovering person is that you may have let these words define you. In this new course, however, seek to hear the words of life that matter to you and build you up, rather than tear you down. Listen to the voices that support where you are trying to go. Hear the words that tell you that you are a fighter, you are courageous, you are committed, you are hopeful, and you are loving. These are the attributes of the person in recovery and the words that matter as you describe who you are. **Deuteronomy 30:19** shares: "*I have set before you **life and death**, blessing and cursing; therefore, choose **life**, that both you **and** your descendants may live.*" When you think about or hear words, they either give fresh life to your spirit or they serve to further kill your spirit. Well, today your task is to know that words matter and the words you need to accept are the ones that give you life. Will the manner in which you live represent the words in your life that matter? Just as you need words of life, those around you need those same words. Let your words matter for the better. Let your words bring life to yourself and to others.

Weekly Questions to Ponder

What are the main thoughts that you took away from this week's devotion?

Is the focus of the devotion a true test for you in recovery?

How can you apply your personal take away from this week's devotion to your recovery this week?

What is a practice you can put into place to help you in this area?

Feeling Drained

Have you ever just been tired of it all? You are dealing with everything under the sun and for the most part you have done well. Yet today, or maybe even for a while, you are feeling drained. It is not simple exhaustion; it is the literal feeling of being dried up. It feels hard to capture the water of life and we are just plain empty. When we feel this way, it can be the beginning of relapse thinking. We do not consciously say to ourselves *I am going back to my addiction*, but our emotions have a way of leading us when we feel empty. In these times of wilderness, we need to see recovery in a different way. It is not seeing the circumstance as being alone with no clear direction, but more of taking the experience as an opportunity to encounter God in a different way. You do not have to be swayed by human activity in your wilderness, but you now open yourself up to the loving God who can water you through this time. Looking in every direction for guidance may not be the way to go. Could it be that maybe you should look *up*? Allow the rain of God to flow down upon you and give you the refreshening you are seeking. It is easy to give in to that dried up feeling believing that there is no more you can do. In fact, that probably is true. Yet, it is God who can do more if you would just allow Him into your dryness. When you are drained, **DIG DEEPER!** If you allow God to water you, like any well, the water can come from deep in the ground or from the open skies. Feeling drained does not have to take you out. Actually, it can be a great opportunity for bringing you in; into the arms of a loving watering God who knows exactly where to bring the water that you need to be filled up again.

Weekly Questions to Ponder

What are the main thoughts that you took away from this week's devotion?

Is the focus of the devotion a true test for you in recovery?

How can you apply your personal take away from this week's devotion to your recovery this week?

What is a practice you can put into place to help you in this area?

Weapons

How are you contending in the fight against your addiction today? What are the weapons you have found most effective in making sure your recovery is sound? It can be difficult when you are trying to destroy an old enemy. The enemy of your addiction has been around for a while, so it feels familiar, comfortable, and easy. When these feelings are stirring around inside of you there does not seem to be any rational reason to fight. Nonetheless, that is the problem because addiction is not rational. The time to bring in greater weapons to destroy old habits must start today. God is our greatest weapon in recovery. By His power He shows us the right people to engage with, the right places to go, the right ways to balance our time. By striving for a greater relationship with Him, God will give us the right marching orders for the fight. In **2 Corinthians 10: 4** we are reminded: "**for the weapons of our warfare are not of the flesh, but divinely powerful for the destruction of fortresses**." When we realize that it is not always a natural battle, we can then be free to give it over to God. Sometimes recovery can feel like a fortress we cannot get past. Yet, the truth is that we need divine intervention to give power to our weapons. So, speak in power, walk in power, pray in power.

Stand ready to fight and give it to God. **He will increase the power of your weapons**.

Weekly Questions to Ponder

What are the main thoughts that you took away from this week's devotion?

Is the focus of the devotion a true test for you in recovery?

How can you apply your personal take away from this week's devotion to your recovery this week?

What is a practice you can put into place to help you in this area?

That's the Job

In our everyday working lives, we may have used the phrase, *That's the job.* We accept the rules and guidelines that have been put in place so that we can perform the required tasks of the job. In some cases, we may accept the way the job is because we do not have any other choice, although we may not like what we must do. In other instances, someone may compliment our work and we may reply with that familiar phrase, *that's the job,* because we feel that we have conquered the expertise needed to do the job well. Whatever the case, we are familiar with doing the work necessary. Yet, in our recovery process can we say the same thing? Do we accept the work necessary to take our recovery to the next level? When you consider your recovery, or someone else comments about it, would one be able to tell that you are doing the job well? Most jobs have specific duties assigned to them and at times you must do *other duties as assigned.* Look at your recovery as something that must be done, but *how* you accomplish the duties is up to you. Being diligent in your quest for recovery will move you forward in your understanding of what it takes to succeed. Why not let God come in and give you the outline of your duties? Seek Him each day for how you can perform the job well. Look for results that you can grasp. As you continue, realize that you have the greatest support you can have in God. He will give you the perfect supervision, rules, and guidelines because *that's the job* and God does it very well.

Weekly Questions to Ponder

What are the main thoughts that you took away from this week's devotion?

Is the focus of the devotion a true test for you in recovery?

How can you apply your personal take away from this week's devotion to your recovery this week?

What is a practice you can put into place to help you in this area?

Grateful and Blessed

There is a sign that may be hanging in your home, or perhaps you have seen it in an office somewhere. The sign reads: *Grateful and Blessed*. What does it truly mean to be grateful and blessed in this recovery process wherein you may struggle? Recovery is not easy. In fact, there may be many days where you feel neither grateful, nor blessed. Nevertheless, it is this mindset in you which produces the gain. In being grateful we take the time to appreciate, not simply what we have, but more so where we have come from. We are not bound by the box of our addiction, but we are liberated to live each day anew. In being blessed we realize that we are no longer at the mercy of our flesh or our emotions, but we are blessed with a clear mind that brings new hope. We are granted God's favor which allows us to proceed forward toward an even better tomorrow. One of the best exercises you can do while in your recovery process is making a grateful list. This does not have to be done just once, but it may be monthly, weekly, or even daily. It is important to take a pause and realize there is much to be grateful for in your life. Along with that the Bible says in **James 5:11a**: "Indeed we call blessed those who showed endurance." This is certainly a road that requires endurance, but God will bless you as you go along this path. As you remain grateful and blessed God will surely help you to endure. Do not just let it be a sign on the wall, but let your life genuinely speak of what it means to be **Grateful and Blessed.**

Weekly Questions to Ponder

What are the main thoughts that you took away from this week's devotion?

Is the focus of the devotion a true test for you in recovery?

How can you apply your personal take away from this week's devotion to your recovery this week?

What is a practice you can put into place to help you in this area?

WAIT

One word that can cause many of us the hardest moments of our lives is the word, ***WAIT***. When you see progress and you feel as if you are finally moving forward, God may say son/daughter, *I need you to WAIT*. What? God, are you kidding me?! I have been doing everything required in my recovery. I have given up things, I have separated myself from the wrong people, and now you are telling me to WAIT?! Emotions spin out of control and all those old feelings run to the forefront of your mind. You get discouraged and believe that things will never work out for you. Right there you need to take a pause. Do you know what the word wait means? ***To wait means to remain stationary in readiness or expectation.*** Too often we give up on our expectations or minimize them because it seems they are just taking too long. However, get yourself ready. Be ready for the overflow of what God wants to do for you. When you allow the discouragement to be greater than the expectation, you may forfeit all that you have worked for to go back to what is easy or familiar. An old song refrain says that 'waiting is the hardest part.' At times it can be, but that does not mean it is not worth every second of the process. So, WAIT with expectation and be ready to receive all that God has for you. Recovery is not a fast process, but it is a growth process. In recovery and in life we all are subject to things we hope will happen for us in our time. What we need to ***expect*** is that what God has for us in His time will be well **worth the WAIT**.

Weekly Questions to Ponder

What are the main thoughts that you took away from this week's devotion?

Is the focus of the devotion a true test for you in recovery?

How can you apply your personal take away from this week's devotion to your recovery this week?

What is a practice you can put into place to help you in this area?

Put it in DRIVE

Most of us are familiar with what it means to get in the car and drive. How mindlessly do we open the door, step in, position ourselves in the seat, close the door, start the car, and put it in drive? It is such a familiar and mindless process that we can do it sleepily. Yet that, in and of itself, can be problematic. We often act mindlessly upon habits that have caused us to be in positions we do not like. It is necessary that we pay attention in recovery. It is not an option to live our days like we are driving a car because, if you think about it, even after we are in **drive** we get into common thought. As a part of transforming our thoughts and behaviors we must be more present even in the small things. I love to drive and could be on the road for hours listening to music and not thinking much about what is happening around me; just going with the flow and the habit of driving. Yet the challenge to each of us is to pay attention to those who are in the cars, trucks, and RVs that surround us. Be careful that you are not the cause of a crash because you were in the mindless habit of driving. Being on the road is a responsibility and being in recovery holds that same responsibility. Do not be the crash agent, or reason that anyone else crashes, because you are a mindless driver; the crash could affect you as seriously as it affects them. So, the next time you step into a car, *wait and remember* that DRIVE is the most serious gear you can move into. In the same way, when you put your recovery in DRIVE do not neglect to remember you have a responsibility for your safety and the next man too. Putting your recovery in **DRIVE** ***means you are in forward motion;*** just make sure that the goal of your motion has a ready mind that is driving toward success.

Weekly Questions to Ponder

What are the main thoughts that you took away from this week's devotion?

Is the focus of the devotion a true test for you in recovery?

How can you apply your personal take away from this week's devotion to your recovery this week?

What is a practice you can put into place to help you in this area?

THE RENEWING

Devotions for the Journey to
Recovery and Life Transformation
Vol. 1

Journal

Renewing Mind Journal:

Renewing Mind Journal:

Renewing Mind Journal:

Renewing Mind Journal:

Renewing Mind Journal:

Renewing Mind Journal:

Renewing Mind Journal:

Renewing Mind Journal:

www.ingramcontent.com/pod-product-compliance
Lightning Source LLC
Chambersburg PA
CBHW071258190726
48292CB00007B/2588